A Walk on the Soft Side

Poems to make Grandparents

by

Gina Claye

*With help from my grandchildren
Nancy, Nell and Bertie Rashleigh-Claye*

© Gina Claye 2021

This book is sold subject to the condition that it shall not, by way of trade or otherwise, be lent, resold, hired out, converted to another format or otherwise circulated without the publisher's prior consent in any format other than that in which it is published.

The moral right of Gina Claye is asserted as the writer.

ISBN 978-1-910779-83-5

Typeset by Oxford eBooks Ltd.
www.oxford-ebooks.com

www.ginaclaye.co.uk

for
Grandparents everywhere

ACKNOWLEDGEMENTS

Grateful thanks to Mary Hartley and friends who encouraged me in this venture.

My grateful thanks to Andy Severn www.oxford-ebooks.com for his skill and humour.

Many thanks also to my daughter, Rachael, who edited it.

And to my grandchildren, Nancy, Nell and Bertie Rashleigh-Claye whose delightful comments and experiences provided me with material for this book.

The Poems

A WALK ON THE SOFT SIDE	9
SNUGGLING UP	11
BARE NECESSITIES	13
NAMING THE FAMILY	15
FEELING ROUGH?	17
GETTING ON WITH IT	19
CRACKING IT	21
DROPS	22
NOT UP TO IT	24
MONEY PROBLEMS	27
NO END TO IT?	29
DON'T DRINK THE BATH WATER	31
PATTER	33
A TANGLE OF DREAMS	35
GRANDDAD'S BIRTHDAY	37
A HUMPY GRUMPY DAY	39
CHRISTMAS EVE	41
IN THE HOME CORNER AT CRECHE	43
PRESENT MEMORIES	45
BACK TO BASICS	47
HAVE I GOT NEWS FOR YOU	48
WARMING UP	51
YOOKING	53
MY BIRTHDAY CAKE	55
RED'S THE COLOUR!	57
STOP THAT !	59
STOP THAT TOO !	61
ROUND THE CORNER	62
COMING HOME	64

There comes a wonderful, almost magic moment, in life when you know that being a grandparent is one of the greatest gifts on earth. I had just arrived; my granddaughter rushed to give me a hug, my daughter handed me a much needed cup of tea and we settled down in the sitting room, watching the little one take her doll for a walk in its new pram.

A WALK ON THE SOFT SIDE

Pushing my pram
with Dolly in,
see you later
we're off to the shop,
But the wheels get stuck
in the cushions
and the arms at the end
make me stop.

You run out of room
on the sofa,
I wish it would go on
a bit more,
But no, I don't want
to get down, Mum,
I'm ever so bored
with the floor.

There's lots of turns
on this walk, Mum
and my feet sort of
slip down the crack,
But Dolly and I
are off now
for a walk on the soft side...
and back.

There's nothing like snuggling up to Granny or Grandad while they read them a bedtime story - all cosy and warm, listening to a favourite story and slowly, slowly drifting off to sleep.

But sometimes they're too wide awake to fall asleep, and they don't see why Granny or Grandad can't go on and on reading to them. "Well, one more story then..." But there comes a point when a glass of wine calls from below. Thank goodness then for teddies, monkeys or any other cuddly toy to take over, and in extremes, a parent.

And there are other times, too, when there is a twitch in your bedclothes and a wriggly body with cold toes, finds its way in...

SNUGGLING UP

Please Granny...
cuddle me up
and hug me snuggly
I can't go to sleep
any more,
I want you to sing to me
tell me a story,
Why are you yawning
and yawning?

I love cuddling up
to you Granny
you're always so warm
and snuggly,
You make me feel safe
when I feel afraid,
you put your arms round me
and hug me.

So please Granny
I'll be ever so good,
if you tell me a story
I won't make a sound,
Cuddle me up
and hug me snuggly,
Cos Mummy says,
It's your turn now.

First thing in the morning it's not unusual to hear my daughter call out, "We've run out of milk. Can you nip up to the corner shop and get some. Oh, and while you're there, get some butter, we're rather low on that." Basic necessities to get the day off to a start. But young ones can have quite a different take on what is the most important thing to put in their mouth first thing in the morning - or at any time.

BARE NECESSITIES

I know you've got
to get milk, Dad
and some apple juice,
And Mummy says
get nappies
and some tea bags too.

Please when you're
in the shop, Dad
get biccit choccit for me
and cake choccit
and ice-cream choccit
so I can have some for tea.

But if the lady
in the shop
says she hasn't got
any for you,
Then please, Dad
remember,
just Choccit will do.

There are many variations of names that grandchildren can give their grandparents. Granny can be Gran, Grandma, Nan, Nana or even a name like Nomy (to rhyme with 'show me') in my case, and Dowy, the grandchildren's paternal granny, and many more. Granddads can be Grandpa, Gramps, Gampy, or just have Grand added in front of their name as in GrandPip, their paternal grandfather.

But as far as the children are concerned, Mummy and Daddy are always Mummy and Daddy... aren't they?

NAMING THE FAMILY

GrandPip is my granddad's name
Dowy is my gran
Nomy is my other gran
my other granddad's – Granddad

One thing I'm sure of,
as sure as can be,
Mummy's always Mummy
Daddy's always Daddy.

But when I was wide awake
last night in bed,
listening to the downstairs sounds
something strange was said

Something that puzzles me
I suppose it always will,
Daddy called Mummy, Rachael
and Mummy called Daddy, Bill.

Children love touching things, exploring them, especially if they haven't come across them before. They see something and want to get their hands on it straight away. Is it soft, hard, dry, wet, cuddly? What's it for? If it's a toy, that's ok. If it's something in the kitchen they know a parent or grandparent will be keeping a watchful eye on them. But now and again they come across something that gives them quite a surprise!

FEELING ROUGH?

— Ow, Ganddad, your chin, it...
— Scratched you?
— Yes, Ganddad, you scatched.

— Ow, it did it again, it...
— Prickled you?
— Yes Ganddad, you pickled.

After being out for a walk or shopping on a cold or rainy day, the children come back to a warm house and the first thing they want to do is get their coat off and their hat and anything else they've been wrapped up in. They want to get on with it, get it all off...

GETTING ON WITH IT

OFF hat
too warm

OFF coat
back home

OFF sweater
there it goes

OFF shoes
time for toes

OFF vest
bare tummy

OFF nappy
Hold ON ...
cries Mummy

Coughs and colds in winter are part of the family scene. In most kitchens or bathrooms there is a cupboard containing the usual medication. But sometimes the answer doesn't lie in unscrewing the top of a bottle and searching the cutlery drawer for a 5ml spoon. Sometimes what is needed is...

CRACKING IT

Mummy get a doctor
  I think I'm very ill,
it didn't work, that deep breath
  though I held it very still.

Mummy get a doctor,
  get her right away
or my horrid, horrid eggcups
  will never go away.

On rainy days, there is still shopping to be done, so I help the little one to put on raincoat and wellington boots, make sure the hood is pulled up and tie on a scarf if it's cold. Walking along the pavement up to the shops we go, avoiding the puddles - well one of us does, the other jumping in them, making as big a splash as possible, enjoying the rain, well mostly...

DROPS

I like raindrops
trickling
down my chin,
but
I do wish
the rain would
STOP
putting
eyedrops in.

From time to time, grandchildren come up with names for things that are very nearly right... but not quite. Sometimes they come up with their own version, especially if it's a four syllable word.

NOT UP TO IT

It's exciting
flying
in an aeroplane,
I'll go again,
I want to.

But I think
I'd find it
ever so scary
going up in a
hairycopter.

We all have money problems at one time or another, so I suppose it's only reasonable that children should have them too. In this case when I say money problems, I mean accessories. While I like to put my money in a shoulder bag, there are some things I'm not sure I'd put my money in...

MONEY PROBLEMS

What shall I put
my money in
to hang on
the pram today?
Perhaps the bag
with the cat on
or the one
with the funny face.

But the one it's already in
is stuck,
I can't get it
off the pram,
so the money
can stay
just where it is,
in my watering can.

I expect we've all tried, at one time or another, to chat to our grandchildren while they're playing, asking them questions, such as, "It's nearly time for your bath. Do you like playing in your bath?" "Daddy's cooking sausages for supper. Do you like sausages?' The last thing a child wants to do when they're totally immersed in a game, is answer stupid questions from grown-ups...

NO END TO IT?

Yes
I
like
chips
and
saussi
and
I
hug
snowbear
and
elphie,
Yes
I
like
eggs
and
baky
and
being
in
my
bath
all
naky.
Stop
asking
me
everythin,
Is
there
no
end
to
it?

Bath time. I love watching them climb into the bath, jumping around if it's a bit hot and then sinking down under the bubbles. There are always a selection of bathroom toys around and I watch fascinated by the way they get hold of them and are immediately absorbed in a game. Sometimes it takes a lot of persuasion at the end of bath time to get them out. I sit there, ready, with a warm towel and a mug of milk but sometimes that isn't what they want...

DON'T DRINK THE BATH WATER

Don't drink the bath water
Stop it, Nell, don't drink it
you don't know what's in it...
I'm in it, Nomy.

That's what I mean
it's not very clean,
**I'm sticking my tongue in,
and licking and licking...**

No, don't drink it
it's scurvy and scummy
and bad for your tummy...
**No, it's not, Nomy,
it's yummy!**

When I finally manage to get them out of the bath, I wrap them in the towel, sit them on my lap and give them a big cwtch (the Welsh word for cuddle). I remember singing, 'This little piggy went to market, This little piggy stayed at home', as I dried their toes. This led to us singing other nursery rhymes, some in English, some in Welsh, as I hugged them dry. And then, of course, they want to have a go all on their own...

PATTER

Think I've got it
Think I know
Think I'll sing it
Here I go

I see thunder
I see thunder
Hark don't you
Hark don't you
Pitter...?
Pitter...?
Peter...
Peter Rabbit raindrops
Peter Rabbit raindrops
I'm wet through
So are you

Sometimes I'm in charge of bedtime. I cuddle them up and read them a story, kiss them goodnight and tuck them up, keeping my fingers crossed that they're drowsy enough to fall asleep. I tiptoe away, listening for any unwanted signs that they're still awake.

On the way to bed that night I creep into their room and watch them sleeping peacefully - such a unique moment; it gives me time to remind myself how precious it is to be a grandparent. I watch them, totally unaware of my presence, in a world of dreams...

A TANGLE OF DREAMS

A tangle of dreams...
A nightly subconscious wish wash
Of daily doings

A tangle of dreams...
Uncurling the coiled connections
Of our mysterious minds

Searching and sifting
As sleeping we drift, in
A tangle of dreams...

Birthdays in the family are always special and Granddad's birthday is no exception: deciding what presents to get him, wrapping them up, planning the birthday cake and of course, making and drawing cards for him. And then there's the question: 'How old is Granddad?'

GRANDDAD'S BIRTHDAY

I've made a card
for Granddad
now the kisses,
let me see,
I had seven kisses
on my card
but Granddad's a lot
older than me

I've done coloured kisses
for Granddad,
they're orange and green
and pink,
I'm counting the kisses
carefully...
got the right number
I think

Mummy's counted the kisses
for Granddad
she says it's right
what I've done,
It's Granddad's
birthday tomorrow
he's going to be
twenty-one.

Now and again comes one of those days when each request or suggestion is met with a grumpy face and, "I don't want to..." Why? Who knows...

A HUMPY GRUMPY DAY

My thumb's got a fumble
my tum's got a tumble
my hum's got a mumble
my mum's got a grumble
  It's a humpy grumpy day

My squash has been squeezed a lot
my choc's mixed with dust and grot
my sausage is much too hot
my crisps have been crushed - by what?
  It's a humpy grumpy day

My head has got toothache
my tooth has got headache
my front has got backache
it's a pain in the neck ache
  And all because
  it's a humpy grumpy day

Christmas Eve. It's all too exciting. Little ones are put to bed, first hanging up their stockings, then told to snuggle down as Father Christmas will only come when everyone is fast asleep...

CHRISTMAS EVE

I've hung up my stocking
I'm all tucked up
but I can't settle down
cos Mummy's still up.

She creeps upstairs
keeps peeping in,
Go to bed, Mum, or
Father Christmas won't come.

If you don't hurry up
it's going to be morning,
Daddy's already in bed
and snoring.

I'd better get up
and go downstairs,
find out what she's up to
'stead of going to bed.

I'll get up now
I'll get up
I will
I ....

At nursery, my granddaughter always made straight for the home corner where she pulled out the teapot, milk jug and mugs to make tea for the dolls, teddies, penguins and monkeys which she sat round a little table. She was away in her own world until she opened one of the cupboards and found something she'd not come across before...

IN THE HOME CORNER AT CRECHE

I've washed all the dishes
put Dolly to bed
and opened the cupboard door,
now I've found something
very strange
I've never seen before.

It's pointed in front
and flat at the back,
don't know what it's for,
it might be a boat
I could sail in my bath,
I've never seen one before.

We don't have one
in our house,
it's not a watering can,
it's not the laptop
which Mummy works
or Daddy's frying pan.

It has a stand
on which it sits
and a handle you can hold,
they say it's useful
but why I don't know,
it's called an iron, I'm told.

I remember seeing my granddaughter for the first time, seeing the tiny being in my daughter's arms. Then holding the tiny bundle myself, feeling incredible happiness at becoming a grandparent.

As months went by, I began to see a likeness here and there of other members of the family...

PRESENT MEMORIES

Sometimes
when you smile,
wickedly,
I see him
in your eyes.
When you look down
I see her as she was
at your age.

But the moment
passes,
and you are you,
unique you,
a meeting
of your mum and dad,
part of us all,
both here
and gone.

In between visits it's good to have a chat on the telephone to hear what they've been up to. After listening to the latest news from the grown-ups, the telephone is passed over...

BACK TO BASICS

— Hello is that Nancy?
— Yes

— Did Daddy give you the telephone?
— Yes

— Have you had your supper?
— Yes

— And your bath?
— Yes

— And you've got your new yellow pyjamas on?
— Yes

— I heard you went swimming last week?
— Yes

— And tomorrow you're going to the zoo to see tigers, giraffes and monkeys?
— Yes

— And what are you doing at the moment?
— Standing up.

One morning I got an email from my daughter which started, "You won't believe this - or perhaps you will…"

HAVE I GOT NEWS FOR YOU

Why are you watching TV?
why are you laughing too?
look at me,
listen to me
Have I Got News For You.

Teddy found the shopping bag
you left in the hall
and he made the milk
and the apple juice
squirt all over the wall.

Then Teddy got hold of the eggs
and the shells all tore
and all the yellow
and jelly bits
went plopping around on the floor.

'You're all wet and sticky,
you're a naughty teddy,' I said,
So I wrapped him
in Mummy's sweater
and put him straight to bed.

I got the brush from the cupboard
and the towel too
and though I've used
all the loo roll
there's still clearing up to do.

So stop watching TV
stop laughing too
look at me
listen to me
Have I Got News For You!

I love hearing my grandchildren telling me their news. "Look what I've been painting... Come and see what I've built in the sitting room... I've got a new dressing gown." They can't wait to tell me about it; the words come tumbling out, well most of them...

WARMING UP

I have a tiger dressing gown
though
I think
the spots are wrong.
But it has
red ears
and makes me
ROAR
each time I put it on

It's big
so it will fit me
for later
when I grow.
But now it's all
SNUGGLY
and WARM,
it's been on the Radi…..
Radi…..
Radi…..o !!!

Grandchildren get up to all sorts. Sometimes it can get a bit tiring and one of the nice things about being a grandparent is you can hand them back at the end of the day...

YOOKING

Yook, I've got peas
on my yap,
Yook, they've rolled
on the floor,
Yet me get down
pick peas up,
Yet me get down
I finished my yunch
don't yike tatoes,
Yet me get down

Yift me up
yet me see
what you doing,
Are you doing cake?
I yike cakes,
make yots of icing
I can yick the spoon,
Yet me see
yift me up
yet me see
what you doing,
I w a n t t o y o o k !!!

One of my duties is to make the birthday cakes. First I have to decide on the shape the cake will take; should I use a round tin or a rectangular one. It depends... if I'm going to decorate it as a swimming pool then obviously not the round tin. If I'm going to do a monkey then two round ones would probably be best.

Over the years I've made many different shapes; there's been a violin, a monster and a baby grand piano with a gorilla sitting on the stool and many more. It all depends what their interests are at the time.

MY BIRTHDAY CAKE

I'm *still* not allowed
in the kitchen
cos they're *still*
making my cake,
When it's done
and no one's around
I'm going to take
a peep.

They've made me an amazing
ballerina cake
cos I love to dance
they know,
Just look at that skirt
it's made of….. wow !
I'll nick a bit now,
they won't know.

I've blown out the candles
Happy Birthday's been sung,
It's been the best
of parties,
I'm sure the rest
of the cake will be fine
but I can't wait to start
on the smarties.

Everyone in the family knows that grandparents are kind and loving and understanding and they agree that grandchildren are the very best thing in the world. But on one very important thing they will never ever agree: Rugby!

RED'S THE COLOUR!

Nomy says to wear
red today
so I've put my red
sweater on,
We've got to hush
when we play downstairs
cos they've got their
iPads on.

They're running up and down
on the iPads,
throwing a funny shaped
ball around,
Then all of them
cheer and cheer
when one of them
dives to the ground.

The ones in red shirts
are winning,
don't think they're
going to fail,
Granddad's in the sitting room
cheering on England
Nomy's in the kitchen
shouting…"Come On Boyos,"
shouting and shouting
for WALES,
….. YEAH !!!

Children are always ready to explore the world, especially the world of grown-ups. I had been about to wash up some of the lunch things that hadn't made it into the dishwasher, when the phone rang. I dumped the washing up liquid on the table and went to answer it. And when I got back...

STOP THAT !

Bertie
STOP
squirting that!
It's meant for
washing dishes

But Nomy
teddy's all dirty
and the dishes
don't mind

Bertie
STOP
squirting that!
It's meant for
cleaning cups

But Nomy
the curtain's all dirty
and the cups
won't mind

Bertie
STOP
squirting that
turn round
and listen to me
W a t c h   o u t ...
OWCH ..... !!!

Then there's the world of the garden to explore: the colours, the scents, picking flowers to go on the kitchen table. In my garden they search for tubes of smarties hidden in the apple tree and in the summer help to pick blackberries for a blackberry and apple crumble. But in their own garden they become a little more adventurous. On one visit I overheard...

STOP THAT TOO !

**Bertie,
STOP THAT!**
But Mummy...

**You shouldn't have got that,
hand it over at once**
But Mummy...

**How on earth
did you get it?**

I got on a chair
I got on the bench
I got it off the wall

**Never ever
get it again**

But Mummy
you got it for Daddy
yesterday...
and the grass needs
a haircut too.

I love going shopping with my grandchildren. Each expedition is an adventure; much better than nipping out on one's own, even if it does take longer. And crossing the road, looking right, left, then right again, because you never know what's round the corner...

ROUND THE CORNER

Careful,
there's a road coming,
I can't see it
but it's there,
it's rumbling
just round the corner,
must hold Nomy's hand
and take care.

I wonder
which road is coming,
not sure which one
it might be,
It might be the slow road
with the red Hackney bus,
Okay, I'll walk sensibly.

Perhaps it's the fast road
with the cars that zoom
or the one
which the bicycles ride,
or perhaps it's the wet one
where the lorries go swoosh,
Yes Nomy,
I'll keep by your side.

It's getting closer
and closer
and I think
I can hear the sound
of the road I like best
in the whole of the world,
Okay, I'll stop
jumping around.

It's coming, it's coming,
it's come,
I can see it
yes I can,
Must hold on tight
but yippee, I'm right,
It's the road
with the ice-cream van.

Saying goodbye after a visit is so, so hard. I watch them standing at the gate waving and I wave back until they're out of sight. Now it's back to everyday life, looking over the photos, marking in the diary when it's time to visit again...

COMING HOME

Nomy's come home,
bags in the hall,
arms outstretched
And I run,
one sandal on,
one sandal off
into her hug.

We swing and slide
in the park,
topple towers of blocks,
throw monkey
back and fore,
Explore stories
together.

Heavy and droopy
I climb on her lap,
hug snuggly,
cuddle into her,
She rocks me,
sings me to sleep.

Where does she go
when she's not with me?
think I've been there
hunting for smarties
in the garden,
Nomy and me.

Why does she go?
cheek wet against mine,
smiling, waving,
The gate clicks,
and there's just me,
Mummy, Daddy and me,
till the next time
Nomy comes home.

www.ingramcontent.com/pod-product-compliance
Lightning Source LLC
Chambersburg PA
CBHW021158080526
44588CB00008B/408